Dualities

First published 2020 by The Hedgehog Poetry Press

Published in the UK by
The Hedgehog Poetry Press
5, Coppack House
Churchill Avenue
Clevedon
BS21 6QW

www.hedgehogpress.co.uk

ISBN: 978-1-913499-27-3

9 8 7 6 5 4 3 2 1

A CIP Catalogue record for this book is available from the British Library.

Dualities

by

Sharon Larkin

Contents

Two Old Sticks..6

Fishing 8

Later..9

August Evening with Lonicera.....................................10

After the Ceremony...11

Nocturne...12

On Not Making a Scene...13

Cactus Bowl...14

Looking for a Spark...15

Mismatch..16

Web...17

Entre Chien et Loup...18

Fowl for Dinner..19

Skulduggery...20

Dreaming..22

Reaching for the Remote..23

Observation..24

Hare Trigger...25

Sprung 26

Waterwalking 27

Clearing Out...28

Wood Pigeon 29

Release 30

Dividing Spoils 31

Two Christmases 32

Snail on a Razor Blade 33

Damselfly Dancing 34

Invisibility Training 35

Another Testing Party 36

Armslengther 38

Mister Mesmer 39

Autumn Colour 40

Therianthrope 41

Rendezvous with Bindweed 42

Fireside Night 43

Mountain Climbing for the More Advanced 44

Hibernaculum 45

Rubber and Leather 46

Variable Geometry 47

Grass 48

Firewords 50

TWO OLD STICKS

Father's is a stocky rod of sturdy wood
with a chunky, non-skid rubber knob.
Bent only slightly, somewhat like a crook
but nowhere near as showy as a crosier.
A good staff for a shepherd; a small shield
tacked on the leading edge and labelled
Cader Idris, a peak he never reached.

Mother's is retractable as love, a thing
she stowed away until she needed it.
The plastic tubes dissemble, masquerade
as wood but don't fool me. They break
apart, threaded through with something
akin to knicker elastic, but a little thicker.
Under pressure, hers feels it might give
way when relied upon, yet extends
in seconds to become a cane to swish
and swash, to correct and collapse again,
signs of existence withdrawn from sight
into a hidden carry pouch, deniable.

I try them both, twirl his while walking
feet akimbo, Chaplinesque. With hook
aloft, it brings high blackberry boughs
with bigger, juicier fruit to hand.
Over rough ground it won't let me down,
even on *Crib Goch,* if I'm brave enough.
Mother's can be whipped out, quick
to hail a cab or wave a person down,
to brandish in a rant or make a point,
poke, prod, trip or thwack a mugger.
The ideal urban accessory.

Standing in the hall today, I view these
walking aids my parents used, want
to dispose of the one less leaned upon,
retain the stick that will serve me best
in years to come, fear I must keep both.

FISHING

There were voles along the river.
In early June, you could hear them
drop into the water as dew began to fall.
She sat next to him then,
eyes fixed on the fluorescent float
bobbing on the surface, waiting for a bite.

She learnt to unhook minnows,
releasing them into his bucket
while he prepared the next bait.
They graduated to gudgeon,
spiny-finned perch, small tench,
avoided deeper water, fearing pike.

Soon she began handling maggots,
enjoying the way they burrowed
into the space at the base of her fingers.
Before long, she was impaling them,
watching the pale liquid first spurt,
then ooze out onto her hand.

LATER

The sting had gone from the sun.
Reddened flesh tightened in the shadows.
A meagre breeze ruffled the willows overhead.
The blackbird at the mill sang in its local accent.
Her young-girl scent mingled with his sweat
in the thickening air.
The parish clock struck nine.
There would be thunder in the night.
Across the brook, a sheep bleat.
Nearby, a gnat whine
and here, a smart slap on a cheek.
One set of footprints in the gathering dew.

AUGUST EVENING WITH LONICERA

Dusk comes to the garden earlier now,
wasps buzz off after a busy dayshift
and it is time for the moths to tremble
as we are drawn to the fire pit.

There is the chink of bottle against glass
as the red is topped up in the glow of coals,
faces reflect the warmth of wine
and words come in small,

loose-tied parcels, inexactly addressed
in the easy fellowship of those who know
each other's disinclination to chatter.
Enough is said, a little too much drunk

and honeysuckle smuggles her scent,
no more than a whisper at the start,
swelling to an insistent stream
as glasses empty, bottles drain.

Even the occasional phrase
falters now, intentions conveyed
only by tendril-touch
and pheromone.

AFTER THE CEREMONY

Still in white, stilettos jettisoned in the sand,
she skips along the beach with her bouquet
in hand, and her man still in his wedding suit.
Newly matched, they strike out along the edge
of the ocean. It glints, ignites the whole coast
on this incandescent June day. Out of shot,
higher up the strand, family and friends stand
around, glasses charged and fizzing, sparking
off conversation as the bride blazes as bright
as a comet might across a velvet midnight sky.
Waves kiss the shore, swish mimicking silk
as her skirts sweep above shell and silicate.
A seabird calls from afar; the pair hurry on,
oblivious to all around them, future bound.

NOCTURNE

The moon slips out from wisps of cloud
to shed a little light on us below.
It's full tonight. Our ghostly shadows

on the path ahead contrive to lead
us to this place and as we kiss
I sense a lunacy behind your face.

It's then I spot the man up there –
seas for eyes, a mouthful of despair.
No sooner seen, he slides again

into a cirrus shroud and I begin
to contemplate the gravity
that tethers earth to satellite,

conclude that it's just fantasy,
this foolish sliding in and out –
a brume that billows in,

pulls back, rolls over once again.
No romance or magic's going on.
It's basic mechanics, Newtonian.

Now it is hard to relax,
to retain perspective. All at once,
parallax starts to play its tricks

and as I recline, *mare, mons*
and man morph into the leer
of a fecund rabbit, a wizard hare.

ON NOT MAKING A SCENE

Room in New York, Edward Hopper, 1932

He couldn't do it anymore, so lost himself
in newsprint while she threatened
one more thud on that bass note.

Outside, down the block, was the antidote
to the acid yellow walls and the door
that was unreasonable: too high, no handle.

His refuge was a bar with tangerine paint.
One more peep from her and he'd punch
his way out of the velvet fist holding him,

as if it was an outsized baseball mitt.
He'd smash the porcelain model
of pale martyrdom, all twisted torso,

tortured saint, with a fracture neglected
since childhood. She had no idea what kind
of day he'd had, how his stock had fallen,

how the adding machine wouldn't compute,
however hard he bashed its keys. She had
no premonition of the flood that was coming

to sweep away her few accoutrements,
the stuff they'd mustered, their cheap art,
the vacant doily screaming between them.

CACTUS BOWL

A full moon, huge in a violet sky,
beams out between rust-hued mesas.
Saguaro giants thrust up in the Sonora,
where the night's obligatory coyote,
head flung back, jaws wide open,
howls at the lemon-yellow moon.

No moon here. She plants her garden
in miniature – opuntia, mammillaria,
scatters grave grit on the bowl's surface.
The desert will flower, barrenness
will be banished in this northern window
where a woman yearns for the golden sun.

LOOKING FOR A SPARK

Long before the affair began, she had dreams
of two houses – one with slates missing,
rain pouring in, ceilings falling;
the other a mansion with extensive wings.

Or sometimes she was alone in a car,
in the back seat, speeding down winding roads,
unable to reach the brake. Or she was a pilot,
out of fuel, approaching a motorway, frantic
for a gap in traffic.

           The night after the infidelity,
she awoke in a sweat, smelt burning, prodded
her other half who grunted, rolled over, took
the duvet with him. She slipped from the bed,
checked plugs, sockets. Found nothing.

After she decided to leave, she lay
next to the snoring mound, imagined
incendiaries flaring, fires licking her feet.

MISMATCH

I didn't want to, but you enticed me out,
found me waterproofs with a hood,
wellingtons only one size too big.

You even warmed me an oversize cardigan
and ski socks on the radiator,
located gloves, and a woolly hat
for me to put on under the hood.

I'd be snug as well as dry.
You thought of everything.
You always did.

Halfway up the hill,
we leaned on a farm gate
to consider the hazy view,
the town spread out below low cloud,
blurred further by rain-lines drawn aslant
and fat raindrops that plopped
from headgear and lashes.

Your face was wet, as was mine.
You had a clean handkerchief,
wanted to dry my cheeks.

I did not want that, turned away
from your kind, proprietorial act.

WEB

A crafty woman has been weaving overnight.
I drag back bedroom drapes, unveil a sheer
fabrication, a tissue of size, swaggering there
at the window. It has snatched dreams, caught
the last breaths of careless callers. We shiver
in the morning air – I inside, outside a cadaver,
a wasp. I wonder if they ever do more than fly,
suck sweetness, pierce flesh, mate, expire.
I turn, watch the duvet as it ebbs and swells
in the light of the low-slung dawn, while still
the corpse lies bundled in its morning jewels.
I admire the dewed threads, abhor the killer-
skill of the insomniac, the bone-white tattoo,
the skull on the back of the false widow.

ENTRE CHIEN ET LOUP

Between thunderstorms,
dog and wolf are facing up
on separate shores.

In its dim mirror,
the lake attempts to make sense
of shapes in the gloom.

Mountains frown, glower
as torrents clatter and dash
their way to the sea.

The house sweats and stews,
throbbing like a red hotel
in the dripping green.

We must chance a snarl
if we are to break the spell
of this plastic trance.

FOWL FOR DINNER

Her goose is cooked. He roasted it himself,
took pride in the act. It was basted with fat
released in the process, squats in its juices.

Still pinnied, he hovers in the kitchen doorway,
trusty corkscrew waving around in one hand,
her Pinot Grigio in the other. He craves red.

'Sauce for the goose must be robust,' he says.
'Equal rights are fine but white wine won't do.
I insist that Merlot's the sauce for the gander.'

SKULDUGGERY

Ossie Rathbone worked for a recruitment agency.
Somebody had to.
As a child, he collected the remains of birds and rodents
his father shot from a bedroom window
but soon began to specialise.

By the time he married Patella,
boxes of skulls she knew nothing about had moved in too.
They filled backlit shelves in their new lounge.
With the main light off, eye sockets and nasal cavities
leered out from the walls, teeth grinned in alcoves,
but it was the pointy bird-beaks that kept her awake
and friends at bay.

Called to local roadkill, Ossie took his spade
to hack off any heads still intact
with a single swipe,
left entrails spilling on tarmac.
Thus his collection grew.

To prevent his wife leaving after new shelves appeared
next to their bed,
Ossie built an extension to house the exotic specimens
he intended to pick up on a business trip to Indonesia,
combined with a little headhunting in Borneo.

Apprehended by security on departing Djakarta,
he escaped detention,
thanks to intervention by the British Embassy
but had to leave a trunk, crammed with scalped skulls,
in the custody of a junior official
with whom he would maintain correspondence.

Back home, he found the extension converted
into a dining room, full of strange people
and a *Come Dine With Me* camera crew.
In the garden a shedload of binbags was awaiting disposal
by the Cleansing Department.

As he howled on his knees
over a fractured skull,
Patella yelled 'You do my head in'
and at last made her move
with a single swipe.

DREAMING

He woke her one morning with tea in bed
as he'd done every day for several years.
'But you're not the one in my dreams,' she said.

He walked away with a shake of his head,
too much of a man for shouting and tears.
He'd wake her next morning with tea in bed.

Each day she would lie there, legs like lead,
no thought in her head about work or careers.
'I know my dream's out there,' was all she said.

'You seem a bit down,' he smiled, patting her head,
'I know what you need: the cup that cheers,'
and he carried on serving her tea in bed.

'You're killing yourself,' the counsellor said,
'It's a slow suicide, just lying there.
Go out and pursue that dream instead.'

Next day she got up, took a bath, dressed in red,
called a taxi and did something mad with her hair,
wasn't there in the morning for tea in bed.
'With the one in my dreams,' was all the note said.

REACHING FOR THE REMOTE

She'd acquired the ability to turn on
the bedroom light without rolling over.
Not odd, you might think,
except, as he knew very well,
she didn't have a bedside lamp
or a cord over the bedhead.

The switch was still on the wall
by the door, three metres away
from his side of the mattress.
Before long, she could open the window
from her bed-ridden position,
let her hand loose around the garden.

It even managed a bit of pruning.
Later she sent it off to the bathroom
for a little wash, its partner following
close behind to wield a scrubbing brush
and heavy-duty nail clippers.
She smiled to hear the *snip, snip, snip.*

This morning they are out the back again,
doing some more target practice.
Their range extends a little each day.
Soon they will be going off
for an adventure on their own.
Soon they'll be going after him.

OBSERVATION

I notice first how your gaze drifts
to the window even though
the blind prevents you
seeing anything out there.

Where before I'd at least get a peck
as you left, I might not now receive
a nod, grunt or sigh. Any of these
would be preferable to nothing.

This Friday night I follow you out,
trail your car, at a distance
so that you don't know what lurks behind
as I keep you in my sights.

You open the passenger door
to settle her into my seat,
are oblivious of my need
to line everything up,

do not hear the crack
as all these things
fall into place,
fall apart.

HARE TRIGGER

I hadn't been looking for him.
My sights were focused on the lake
hoping to catch a swallow mid-skim.

My mind wandered to yesterday.
I hadn't been expecting you either,
dropping in at the wrong moment.

I failed then, and fail now, sigh,
detach myself from the eyepiece.
Only then do I spot the bounder,

haunching it down the bank
coming to a halt, then turning
to face me, the obliging poser.

Again, I think of you, crashing in,
finding me otherwise engaged,
mid-act, in fact, the air crackling.

Seconds pass. Time freezes.
We make eye contact, I stoop
to the tripod, refocus, shoot.

SPRUNG

She had to get out of there.
There was no give in those
walls of terrible celadon.

She was packing them out,
pressed up hard against
them, probing for a nook

to poke, a spot to prod,
testing for a weakness
but everything was hard.

There was no elasticity,
no ease, and still she swelled
and swelled and swelled.

Something had to yield.
The imperative to wax,
the urge to push

brooked no refusal.
The green prison had
to split and let her leaf.

WATERWALKING

She'll have to be brave to get out of the boat
and not look around at the waves that rage.
She must keep her eyes on what seems to float.

Thudding in the chest, tightness in the throat
are to be expected at this desperate stage
but she'll have to calm down, get out of the boat.

Financial incentives, big cheques and large notes
will not work, nor the bribe of a generous wage.
She'll just have to bank on what stays afloat.

No atlas or manual, no maxims or quotes,
it's far too late to read *one more page.*
She must go untutored and get out of the boat.

No time for words that someone else wrote,
a mentor's advice, the wisdom of a sage.
She must stay focused on what keeps afloat,

yell out all the things she's learned by rote,
rattle the bars of Leviathan's cage.
Come on, woman of valour, get out of the boat.
Set your face, fix your eyes on what's still afloat.

CLEARING OUT

On the pavement, she waits for a taxi.
The sun shouldn't be this strong in November,
after last night's storm and floods
but a gentle breeze pats her cheek,
ruffles her hair like an encouraging aunt.

Her eyes close. She needs to sleep.
Flashes of blood and fuchsia
suffuse the inside of her lids
but the liver-coloured blot remains
in the centre, keeps drawing her focus.

She tries distraction, tunes into sounds:
terrier yaps nearby, a distant tractor,
sparrows chirping in the pyracantha,
but memories of bawling lips
inches from her face, drown out everything.

The cab stops. Her eyes open.
Without looking up at the window
where a figure bobs back behind a curtain,
she slips into the car, is driven away.

WOOD PIGEON

The last removal lorry groans away,
housecleaners find the ring
she thought she'd lost, and she's left
in the front garden
with door and car keys.

There's no twittering
from the dunnocks
in the forsythia this morning
but she knows they're there.
There's the odd fluttering.

She steadies herself against the porch
and takes three deep breaths,
hears him in the neglected leylandii
in the back garden
she is abandoning for good.

You, poor fool.
Yeah you, poor fool.
Yeah you, you poor fool.
You.

RELEASE

The morning of the affidavit
he pulled back the curtains
to find sooty mould had grown
overnight on his prize opuntia,
peered closer to note that the dark fuzz
had an ugly face, pulsated when prodded,
threatened to impale itself, become a fixture.

Already late to swear the oath,
he Googled *bat*, checked rules
pertaining to handling the species,
consulted bodies on how to remove this one
without turning it into a corpse.

Gardening gloves, brush and dustpan
were accessories to his act.
He disentangled the blinking thing
to transfer it to the outside world
where he expected it to flop
around for a bit ... then flit off.

DIVIDING SPOILS

Only after waving goodbye
to the old microwave, do I stop
to look at the handbook left behind.

I'd forgotten the oven came
with a probe to poke in any dish,
to give a rough idea of the heat inside.

The gauge still skulks on the shelf
above the grimy film that betrays
where the appliance once stood.

Elsewhere squares of pale carpet sigh
where weight once bore down on them
but they are not bouncing back.

Upstairs the memory foam mattress
still whispers of your tendency to lie
on your right. I can make out

the jut of hipbone, thrust of buttock.
Down there, your feet warmed mine.
Here on the pillow, a hair, and alas

your essence still teases the air.
In my hand, a manual in gibberish
that insists I read and reread it

though the gadget is long out of juice.
Any kit has functions we pay extra for
but never learn how to use.

TWO CHRISTMASES

i

He dragged out last year's tinsel,
buffed up scuffed baubles,
sneezed as he dangled them
on the dusty branches,
stroked the fairy's thighs
as he spread the folds
of her yellowed dress
and straightened the wand,
sat down to microwaved turkey
with some of the trimmings,
forgot the day with wine.

ii

He asked his neighbours
for a bough of the conifer
that darkened his garden,
made paper angels to fly on it,
wrote a card to his ex-wife,
delivered it in person,
worried her with a smile,
popped into the drop-in centre,
served down-and-out dinners,
sang them some carols,
forgot about the wine.

SNAIL ON A RAZOR BLADE

She has a penchant for life on the edge,
abode never quite fixed, travels light,
takes the refuge of last resort–
her fragile, backpack-bivouac.
Soon crushed, her soft flesh oozes
with the invitation to abuse.

He's a sharp character, edgy,
always ready to slice a nemesis
with his ever-present shiv.
Their meeting seems inevitable.
She slinks herself along the length
of his blade. It slits. She feels herself

split. This is self-harm par-excellence.
Her whole body's on the line.

DAMSELFLY DANCING

They are in hold, tarsus to tarsus,
maintaining a seemly distance
between thorax and abdomen.

This is a ball, where phantasm leads,
lifts his damsel, or seems to
undergird her pokerish body.

He is rapt,
attentive to her alien head.
Her mandible mercifully turns

away from us – voyeurs of a stalled
romance. One move from us
and they'll decouple, she will fly,

he will fade, taking his stoop
and humeral stripes with him
into some parallel universe.

Alas, she has imagined him,
dreamed up touchpoints,
read too much into a spectre,

fancied him as soulmate
of similar provenance, failed
to register difference.

But hush. Don't move. Prolong
the moment. Allow the shade
to frog-prince into reality.

INVISIBILITY TRAINING

There's a lot to be said for
being an outsider inside,
flat against magnolia emulsion,
sniffing the chemical make-up
of the room, the taste of another's
scent settling on your lips,
snatches of indiscretion filing themselves
in your braincells, as moths
from unfamiliar closets hover
like mini drones above your hair.

Someone's bemused smile scans
your alcove, trying to make out
your outline above the vol-au-vent
the observer is about to pop
between their lips.
Now your index finger taps out
Morse on the Dulux behind you.
Three short stabs, three long, three short.
Pause, repeat. Pause, repeat.

You turn to take a virtual snapshot
of the dark street through a sliver
in the blind, where a man
staggers, gropes for support
from a low brick wall.
Drunk or sick perhaps.
The symptoms look the same
to a distant stranger.

Your pupils return to the room.
The silent inquisitor has moved on
like a puff of cloud on a breeze.
Everyone else merges into blown vinyl.

ANOTHER TESTING PARTY

It's too easy to be one of the out-crowd,
one of the unclean, skulking in the kitchen
or squatting on the fourth stair from the bottom
with a mousy misfit, sharing the sherry bottle
while you're glancing sideways
at the chemically enhanced specimen
shimmering under the glare of downlight,
attracting all kinds of insect life,
like a honey jar at a picnic.
The flight imperative tussles
with the fight instinct,
that urge to stick up a pair
of belligerent fists, manicured, naturally.

A balcony's a good retreat, promising intrigue,
secrets to be shared with another pariah.
Or there's the low sofa in the anteroom,
where too many lasses with various degrees
of anxiety disorder are shoe-horning rears
into too few inches of vacant Dralon,
where they might wallow in a stew
of fellow-female hormones,
discussing the merits of cross-stitch and stumpwork,
preferences for punch needle, crewel thread,
prejudices for Anchor, DMC, Madeira.

Then, the struggle to squirm out of the clutches
of the cosy oestrogenous zone
to track down another Baileys, or to let some out,
only to discover that some sister-usurper
has slithered into your spot
while you were replenishing or evacuating.

Time to totter to a patio,
stagger to a summerhouse,
slope off anywhere but there.

ARMSLENGTHER

They are all on the run in some fashion
even if it's only pyjamas they're sporting.
She is not the static entity you imagine
as she cowers in crooks of sofas, busy hugging cushions.

It takes a lot of energy to resist opening a door,
or to slam it shut, heaving her whole bodyweight
against it, Kevlar-ing her core against inevitable onslaughts
while a little well-wisher, all smiles

and how-are-yous-without-the-question-marks,
sidles in through the back door.
Now, the running truly begins. She makes them tea,
invites them to perch at the far, far end

of her chaise-très-très-longue,
having pre-rendered armchairs unusable
with piles of paperwork, interspersed
with knitting needles, points outermost,

last night's plate, fork, and knife, brazenly
balancing her leftovers on the toppling heap.
She answers her visitor's questions with lies,
keeps them guessing

which one of her they're talking to today,
assumes her duplicitous caller's doing likewise.
She surveys them with her best stare
until they squirm on her worn moquette,

hastening their retreat. And all the time,
her hands are doing their phantom knitting,
head switched to *Escapologist,*
legs paused in *Marathon* mode.

MISTER MESMER

We have orchestrated this:
a soirée for two enthusiasts
to share a mutual passion.
Kindred spirits, if you like.

One look from your Merlinesque eyes
releases my normally-broken tongue,
banishes diffidence, liberates banalities,
so I witter like a pea-brained extrovert.

But suddenly I'm poleaxed by hypnosis,
stunned utterly mute as you execute
your pupil power.

As if under a spell
I knot your tie around
your tenderness,
lead you to a futon.

AUTUMN COLOUR

That October afternoon
a hasty arrangement
to take a half-day off
travelling separately
to our venue.

I hadn't expected to find
the front door unlocked,
your grey suit, white shirt,
abandoned on the stairs
and you, already between
burgundy silk sheets,

me, regretting the greyness
of my celibate underwear,
already hurrying out of it.

THERIANTHROPE

I never knew what I would be getting.
Every time you showed up in a fresh outfit
as if experimenting with a new wardrobe.
Each combo came with a different persona,
a whole tribe of them.

The success in the city in pin-stripes,
preppy loafer in argyle sweater,
hipster in lumberjack shirt,
shapeless shorts ... and sandals,
for heaven's sake.

And then, the rocker in black leather,
heaven help me.
Yes, I liked that look best
but found it hard not to snigger
when you creaked at sleeve and knee.

It wasn't until you'd shown me everything
that the filters across my lens proved a distortion.
All versions had been blurry reflections,
two dimensional, temporary, untrue.
Naked, you were magnificent.

RENDEZVOUS WITH BINDWEED

After dark, on the outskirts of the copse
a twig snapped for no reason except
that I heard it, and the white trumpet

on the fence might have trembled
at the sound, as a chill breeze flushed
insects from the sheltering cone, left

the stigma unassailed, to sing laments
to the virgin ... and the green heart
might have blanched, convulsed,

or a tendril recoiled as if brushed
by the hand of an uninvited lover.
But I saw none of these, sensed them

only as the twitch of a leveret's ear,
the settling down of a tawny feather,
a moth wing's folding, thus ...

There was no tug at my feet from the earth
as I crept close, kept tryst with the pale herald
at the wood edge at moonrise.

FIRESIDE NIGHT

You bring back a sack of sticks,
twigs to toss on the embers, a gesture
to prolong warmth, delay the dark.

We start at every spit and spat,
quick to extinguish sparks that, left to smoulder,
would ruin the hearthrug,

even set the house on fire.
Dawn finds us sitting with the ashes,
still side by side, still talking.

You lift your head from my shoulder.
The flames have done their work,
lasted long enough to help us remember,

to see pictures that kept us from slumber,
cause us now in the stark and morning light
to be up and out, seeking fresh kindling.

MOUNTAIN CLIMBING FOR THE MORE ADVANCED

Masterful. That is the only word
to describe your leadership tonight
and yes, I had heard and feared
your reputation ... but it's all right.
You couldn't aspire to such ascents
or inspire me to reach such levels
without acquiring wide experience.
So as you take me on your travels
to unfamiliar places, on expeditions,
I go as a pupil, you as the master,
and as I come, I trust my intuition
to submit to you as a kind of sherpa.
See, whichever peak we aim for now
another's always coming into view.

HIBERNACULUM

We are at ease with us.
No need for airs, grooming, clothes.
These winter nights
there is the scent of mammal.
We burrow in our mound,
wear each other as pelt.

RUBBER AND LEATHER

Her pink ribbed hottie flops unstoppered,
trickling its last drops into the bath
over the off-white rim, and with a little laugh,
she finds she is thinking of him.

Later she notices him
taking longer than necessary
plumping up his cushion before slumping,
with a little sigh, into well-worn leather
and she is wondering whether
he is thinking of her.

VARIABLE GEOMETRY

After the flight of youth
comes the fixed wing of family life,
a grounding.

When they, in turn, have taken off,
it's time to assess the craft
for airworthiness.

There are likely to be dry joints, seizings,
restricted airflows, signs of fatigue,
hydraulic leaks.

Swing wings might no longer do so,
flaps may have become
floppy.

Watch for lateral movement ... drift,
sagging.
Taking off begins to seem unwise.

GRASS

It covers our bald spots
as a hairweave might
but unlike a cosmetic act,
it does so spontaneously.
Those so inclined
might say miraculously.

You can help it along
if you till and condition the soil,
select well-suited seed
for climate and lie of land,
sow, water, and after seedsprout,
when sward has established itself,
keep it trimmed, weed free, fed.

Or you can import turfscalps
to graft onto your earthpate
if you wish to cheat.

But in a conducive medium
in a supportive environment
such as this rain-blessed patch
of western British loam,
grass will simply come
to make its home unbidden
where rocks, trees and lakes
have failed to colonise,
where spoil from excavation
has done no damage to the land.

After years in this place,
we praise the lawns, robes
that have covered our nakedness,
each blade as it has submitted
to our blades, and yet has stayed
and asked for more.

FIREWORDS

We struck vestas to light the fire.
It went out repeatedly
until ignition seemed to come
from somewhere other than our own hands
and then the firewords caught.

Now we must watch over them,
attend to the flame
or the firewords will falter,
our house will stay cold
and red-letter days cool to black.

So we rise early each morning
to lay the hearth, make a bed
for the firewords, their crimson font.
And we stay up late at night
to settle the embers before sleep,
bedded down between soft covers.

We question the need
to take so much care, suspect
it could all be less of a chore,
but the effort is necessary,
for firewords are also bright children,
hot with promise and rare reward.

Birthed in years of vigour
into our fumbling hands,
the firewords grow, become armour,
protective in old age.

Forged in the labour of fire,
the fire of labour,
they flare up in the ardour
of attentive parents,
come to rest in a child's innocence.

ACKNOWLEDGEMENTS:

Fishing was included in the prizewinners' anthology *May Day* published by Cinnamon Press (2013) and included in the anthology *Beyond the Well-Mapped Provinces* produced by Cheltenham Poetry Society (2013).

Later was published on-line as Summer Evening Sounds by *Clear Poetry* (December 2015).

Nocturne appeared on-line with the title Pareidolia in Rat's Ass Review's *Love & Ensuing Madness* collection (May 2016).

Cactus Bowl was published in *Perspectives*, the magazine of Cheltenham Arts Council (January 2015).

Mismatch was published on-line by Clear Poetry and included in the subsequent anthology (December 2015)

Web was published with the title Caught in a Web in the anthology *Maligned Species: Poems on Spiders* by Fair Acre Press (February 2016).

Fowl for Dinner was published in *Prole* magazine (December 2018)

Reaching for the Remote was published in *Prole* magazine (May 2017)

Sprung was published in the Transition edition of *Here Comes Everyone* magazine from Silhouette Press (September 2016)

Snail on a Razor Blade was published on-line by The Mouse (August 2016).

Damselfly Dancing appeared in the prizewinners' anthology *In the Cinnamon Corners* published by Cinnamon Press (October 2017).

Autumn Colour was published on-line in Rat's Ass Review's *Love & Ensuing Madness* collection (May 2016).

Therianthrope was published on-line by Clear Poetry with an audio recording on SoundCloud (October 2016)

Firewords was included in the prizewinners' anthology *In the Cinnamon Corners* published by Cinnamon Press (October 2017).